25 Just-Right Plays for Emergent Readers

BY CAROL PUGLIANO-MARTIN

SCHOLASTIC
PROFESSIONAL BOOKS

NEW YORK • TORONTO • LONDON • AUCKLAND • SYDNEY

To Scott,

who is

"just-right"

for me.

Cover design by Jaime Lucero
Cover illustration by Larry Daste
Interior play illustrations by Ellen Joy Sasaki; activity illustrations by James Graham Hale
Interior design by Kathy Massaro

ISBN: 0-590-18945-X
Copyright © 1998 by Carol Pugliano-Martin
All rights reserved.
Printed in the U.S.A.

Contents

Celebrate the Seasons

Exploring Nature

All About Animals

Plays for Anytime

Introduction

I recently spoke to a primary school teacher who told me that many of his students enjoy reading stories aloud. So he began to adapt stories into plays by creating scenes with speaking parts for his students to play. I thought that his task, while very admirable, seemed like a lot of work for a busy teacher. And that is how this book came about. This collection of original plays is specially tailored for emergent readers. All you need is a copy machine and some eager children!

These plays do not require building sets, making costumes, or putting on productions. Instead, they offer an easy and inviting way to use the form of plays as a tool for helping young children enter the exciting world of reading.

There are 25 reproducible plays in this book, based on favorite primary themes that children adore, such as seasonal celebrations, animals, and the natural world. Some of the features and benefits of using these plays follow.

❀ Each play is easy to read, using words from leveled word lists. Some plays use simple and fun made-up words that will help children discover the playfulness of language.

❀ The plays use devices such as rhyme, repetitive language, and predictability to help young children gain confidence as readers and take pleasure from the experience of reading. Appealing illustrations are an aid to comprehension.

❀ Sentences are short for easy reading and most do not run beyond one line. Type size is large for emergent-reader eyes.

❀ The number of speaking parts in each play ranges from two to enough parts for the whole class. Many plays can be adjusted to use fewer or more speakers as you see fit. You may also wish to have students team up to read the same part together.

❀ Many plays are based on real-life situations, which helps children to connect reading to their daily lives.

❀ Reading these plays aloud provides a less competitive, less stressful environment for emergent readers. Plus, research has shown that reading aloud helps oral language development, an important element in emergent reading.

❀ In addition to the plays, there is a simple-to-do extension activity for each play (see pages 6 to 14) that will help you to integrate your students' play-reading experiences across the curriculum.

You may find these tips helpful as you use this book with your class:

BEFORE READING THE PLAYS

❀ Photocopy the play and distribute a copy to each student. Also, write the play on chart paper, so you can point along as children read aloud.

❀ Divide speaking parts into smaller or larger groupings as desired. For example, three children might read the same part.

❀ After assigning parts, hand out crayons or markers so that children can highlight their lines. This will make it easier for children to identify their own parts as they read.

❀ Read the play aloud to your class before they read it on their own. This will help to familiarize children with the play's content and action. Go over vocabulary that might be new to students.

WHILE READING THE PLAYS

❀ Incorporate phonics lessons into play readings. For example, you might challenge children to find all of the words in a play that begin with /b/.

❀ Ask children to identify rhyming language or repeated refrains.

❀ Divide the class into reading groups to read different plays together. Each group can work independently and then come together as a class to share their reading.

❀ Invite children to act out the plays using simple paper-bag or stick puppets to portray different characters. Using a puppet behind a simple stage will help to create a feeling of safety and anonymity for children who may feel uncomfortable performing in front of a group. (You can make an instant stage by covering a table with a floor-length tablecloth and having children crouch behind it.) Give children the option to read from their scripts while performing, or to memorize their lines, if they prefer.

AFTER READING THE PLAYS

❀ To assess comprehension of the plays, ask follow-up questions after reading.

❀ Encourage children to write their own plays. One way to start is by inviting students to write "What Happened Next?" episodes that continue the plays.

❀ Have children take home copies of the plays to read with family members.

❀ Put on simple productions of the plays as presentations on Visitors' Day.

I hope you and your students will discover the joy of words, reading, and drama through the plays in this book!

Carol Pugliano-Martin

Curriculum Connections

CELEBRATE THE SEASONS

Time for Fall

ALL FALL DOWN

Invite students to stand up and pretend they are leaves about to fall off a tree in autumn. Have them talk about how they feel. Then, invite students to pretend they are slowly falling to the ground. They can make noises if they wish. What kind of sounds might a falling leaf make? Later, ask students how they felt to be falling leaves. Did they feel like the leaves in the play? Have they ever been afraid of trying something new, only to discover that the experience was fun? Ask students to share their experiences.

Autumn Sounds

GUESS THAT SOUND

Play a "Guess That Sound" game with your class. Invite children to pick a sound that they would like to try to simulate. They can choose crunching leaf sounds from the play or pick any other sound. Provide materials and containers for the children to make their sounds. (boxes, tissue paper, brushes, combs, pennies) For example, place dried beans or rice in a covered shoe box. When shaken, it makes a good rain sound. As one child shares his or her sound, have the rest of the class, with eyes closed, guess what sound the child has simulated. Then, challenge students to guess what the child is using to make that sound.

Snowflakes

COOPERATIVE SNOWFLAKES

Invite children to make their own sparkly snowflakes. Use a paper plate or large round lid to trace several circles on old file folders. Cut them out to make circle templates. Have students trace and cut out circles from light-colored construction paper. Next, let students brush on "ice crystals"

(a mixture of 3 tablespoons salt and 1/4 cup warm water). Let the papers dry overnight. The following day, have students fold and cut their circles as shown to make snowflakes.

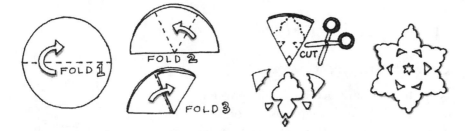

Chances are, most of the children's snowflakes will look different from one another's. Use this opportunity to relate their snowflakes to those in the play. Do any look like flowers? Do any look like stars? Later, place all of the snowflakes on a bulletin board in a snowman shape to illustrate the point of the play: even though all of the snowflakes look different, when they are put together, they can make a snowman. Begin a discussion on how this concept can apply to the class as a whole. How can children in the class, like the snowflakes, cooperate to achieve the same goals?

Groundhog Day

SPREAD THE NEWS

Celebrate Groundhog Day by reading or performing this play, using whichever ending applies. Then make a mock television newscast of the outcome. Invite students to play the newscaster, reporters on the scene, people being interviewed about the event, and the groundhog. Begin by having the newscaster tell television viewers what happened when the groundhog came out of its burrow. Then have the reporter interview the groundhog by asking, "How do you feel after [seeing/not seeing] your shadow today?" Next, have another reporter interview people about what they think about an early spring or six more weeks of winter. End with the newscaster wrapping up the story in the "TV studio."

Hooray for Spring!

SPRINGTIME POETRY

What are some signs of spring where you live? Ask students to name some of their favorite things relating to this season. Then write their responses on the board. Using all of the class suggestions, write a poem together about their favorite spring things. Copy the poem onto a large piece of chart paper and display it on a bulletin board. Invite children to draw or paint pictures to accompany the poem. Read the poem aloud together on the first day of spring to celebrate its arrival!

EXPLORING NATURE

From Seed to Plant

GROW, SEED, GROW

Help children construct "see-inside" growing containers to get a close-up look at a seed's underground growth. Cut two slits in a paper cup as shown. Fold down the cut panel, and tape plastic wrap over this opening. Then fold the cut panel back up again. Place a rubber band around the cup to hold the panel in place. Use a pencil to make a hole in the bottom of the cup, fill the cup with soil, and plant one or two dried lima or kidney beans near the panel. Place on a tray and keep the soil moist. To view their seeds, students remove the rubber band and pull down the panel.

Encourage children to make daily observations of their seeds and to note changes. Have them start a plant diary in which they pretend to be their sprouting seed. Ask children to make daily entries describing what is happening to the seed and how it feels about these changes. Ask for volunteers to share their entries. Are the seeds growing at different rates? Discuss how plants are similar to people in that they all grow at their own pace!

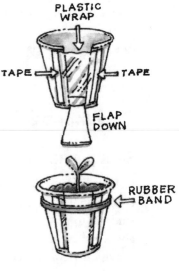

Sunflowers

MAKE SUNFLOWER MASKS

To enhance children's play-reading experience, let students don sunflower face masks. Provide children with large yellow paper plates and help them cut out eye and mouth holes. Then hand out unshelled sunflower seeds, glue, and yellow and orange paper. Invite students to glue seeds around the center of the plate, and to glue cutout paper petals around the plate's rim. Show them how

to tie the masks on with string. For more fun, invite students to make "bees" out of cotton balls and construction paper scraps. Students can cut out tiny features and glue them onto the cotton balls to make bee faces and antennae. Invite the "sunflowers" to wear their masks during readings of the play, while the "bees" go visiting from flower to flower.

Me and My Shadow

SHADOW PUPPET PLAYS

After reading the play, discuss ways shadows look different from the objects that make them. (A shadow is flat and shows the outline of an object, but not its features.) Then let children explore the science behind shadows as they produce plays with shadow puppet performers. Have children make simple puppets out of cardboard. They can poke holes for eyes or use scissors to snip out other features, then tape the puppets to rulers or unsharpened pencils. Make a simple stage by cutting an opening in a large box and taping pieces of waxed paper across the opening to make a screen. Darken the room and shine a lamp behind the screen. Have students hold their puppets between the light and the screen. Suggest that they move their puppets closer to and farther from the light to explore different effects.

Stormy Weather

STORM SOUNDS

Ask children to name different kinds of weather and list these on a chart. (rain, hail, wind, thunder) Go down the list, asking, "What different sounds do you hear during each kind of weather?" Record responses. Then, divide the class into groups—one group for each kind of weather on the list. Invite the groups to take turns presenting sounds for their weather type. Encourage children to notice not only the kind of sound being made, but also the way the sounds are made. For example, you can ask the observers, "Were the wind group's sounds quiet or loud? Why do you think this group made the wind sound that way?"

Neighbors in Space

PICK A PLANET

Ask students to choose one of the planets or the sun and invite them to learn more about it. Children can look at picture books or consult a librarian for help with their research. After they have learned new facts about their planet or the sun, change the play to include the new information. Read the play as a class so that everyone can learn the newfound facts.

ALL ABOUT ANIMALS

Get Set for a Pet

PET POLLS AND GRAPHS

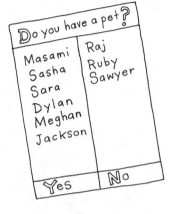

Do you have a pet?

Masami	Raj
Sasha	Ruby
Sara	Sawyer
Dylan	
Meghan	
Jackson	
Yes	No

Take a pet poll in your class. Begin by asking, "Do you have a pet?" and help children make a simple bar graph, with a Yes and a No column, to record their responses. Help students interpret their data by asking, "Which column has the most names in it?" "How many children in our class have pets? How many do not?" Then take additional polls and make more graphs by inviting children to pose other pet questions, such as, "What Kinds of Pets Do You Have?" "How Many Pets Do You Have?" or "What Pet Do You Wish You Had?" Ask questions such as, "Do more children in our class have dogs or fish?" "How many pets do we have altogether?" "Which pet do most children wish they had? How do you know?"

Guinea Pig Song

CLOSE-UP ON PETS

This play is about children observing their classroom pet. Is there a pet in your classroom? If so, help students hone their observation skills and express their observations through speaking or writing. Invite your class to observe the pet closely. Encourage them to notice how and what the pet eats. Have they seen the pet sleep? Does the pet play? What does it like to do? If there is not a pet in your classroom, ask children to imagine one that they might like to have. The pet can be a real animal or a make-believe one. Instead of observing an actual animal, children can do research by reading simple books, looking at pictures, or using their imagination to identify a make-believe pet's characteristics and habits.

New Frog in the Pond

FURTHER FROG POND ADVENTURES

Ask children to imagine what might happen with the frogs after the play ends. What other things might the frogs do together? What kinds of adventures might they have? Use children's responses to add another scene or several scenes to the play. After reading your new frog play together, ask, "What things might you do to help someone new to your neighborhood feel welcome?" Use this information to write a new play together about a child who is new to their neighborhood.

A Duckling Tale

ALL IN A LIFE CYCLE

As a class, research the life cycle of a duck from egg to adult. Then make a class circle-shaped mural depicting each stage in the process. Afterward, ask, "What other animal's life cycle would you like to find out about?" Record children's responses, then divide the class into groups based on their choices. Help each group research their animal and make a circle-shaped mural about it. Display the murals and help students compare them. Ask: "How is a [dog's] life cycle different from that of a duck? How is it the same?" Depending on the types of animals chosen, this can be an opportunity to discuss the differences among mammals, birds, amphibians, reptiles, and fish.

Fish School

RULES TO LIVE BY

After reading the play, see if your class can come up with other rules the fish school may have. Use this discussion as a springboard to ask children to come up with their own set of class rules. What are some things the class can do to keep themselves orderly? Some examples may include: talking out problems, not hitting, raising your hand to speak, etc. Invite children to work in teams to write and illustrate their ideas on tagboard or sturdy paper. Then join the pictures to make a banner and display it in a prominent place in the classroom so that it can be referred to all year long.

Ready to Fly

COMINGS AND GOINGS

Explain to students that some animals migrate—move from place to place—to find better weather and more food. Most travel to warmer places in winter and then return to their original habitat in the spring. Pick a bird in your region that migrates and consult a field guide to birds to find out about its migratory route and destination. Plot the bird's migration route on a map. Then, learn about other migrating birds and plot their courses as well. One unique bird to learn about is the arctic tern. This bird migrates from the North Pole to the South Pole and back, flying halfway around the world twice a year! To take your class's migration studies further, help students find out about other migrating animals, including ladybugs, bats, salmon, caribou, and butterflies.

D Is for Dinosaur

GOING ON A DIG

Explain to students that scientists called archaeologists dig for dinosaur bones and other relics of the past. Create your own dig site and invite your class to become amateur archaeologists. Fill large boxes or dishpans with dirt or sand. Bury everyday objects in the boxes (buttons; shells; rocks; clean, cooked chicken bones; paper clips) without letting the children know what you've buried. Let students use plastic spoons and old paintbrushes to dig up and dust off the objects, and then have them write stories about the items they found. Tell them to pretend that they've never seen these things before. Encourage them to create a history around the object and give it a new name based on its characteristics or possible uses.

PLAYS FOR ANYTIME

Pop! Pop! Popcorn!

POPCORN PANTOMIMES

Give your students an opportunity to listen to popcorn popping—and munch it! You can either use a popcorn popper or pop it the old-fashioned way—by heating it in oil in a pan on the stove. Invite students to describe what they hear (at first, there are just a few pops; the popping then builds as the kernels pop more rapidly, and then the popping sounds peter out as fewer and fewer kernels are left). Then, invite students to pretend they are kernels of popcorn popping, starting out with a pop now and then, then getting more and more frequent, and gradually popping less and less. Have students take turns playing the *pip!* kernel. When the *pip!* kernel pops up, have that child choose a different movement from the rest of the class to distinguish that kernel from the others.

Big, Bad Cold

BE WELL, STAY WELL

After reading the play together, encourage your class to contribute pages to a "How We Stay Healthy" big book to keep in your classroom all year. Ask students to suggest things they can do, not only to prevent a cold, but to stay healthy in general. Some suggestions may include: wash your hands often; cover your mouth and nose when sneezing or coughing; exercise; eat plenty of fruits and vegetables, etc. Then, have students write and illustrate their ideas and bind the pages together with "O" rings.

Loose Tooth

TOOTH TALES

Create a chart on classroom tooth loss. List all of the children's names on the chart. Then write how many teeth, if any, each child has lost. As students lose teeth throughout the year, invite them to update the chart. If possible, take a photograph of each child as he or she loses a tooth. Hang the photos near the chart. Then take a photograph after the child's new tooth has grown in. Place it next to the lost-tooth photo. Invite children to share tooth-loss stories and what rituals, if any, take place in their family when they lose a tooth. If you can remember a story of your own, share it with your class.

Time for the Party!

STORYBOOK BIRTHDAY

Choose a favorite character from a book your class has read together. Then plan a birthday party for that character. Ask children to consider what they would need for the party. Who should be invited? What kinds of presents or decorations would the character like? Then set a time to have the party. Set the book on a chair in place of the character or invite students to draw pictures of the character and display these on a bulletin board. Let children make cards and presents for the character, or draw pictures of the kinds of presents they would bring. Serve food, choosing treats the class is sure the character would like!

The Name Game

GETTING TO KNOW YOU

This play can come in handy as a name-learning game for the beginning of the school year to help children (and you!) learn one another's names. After children have read the play using their own names, invite them to pair up and insert their partner's name in the play instead. For example, "Her name is _____. That rhymes with _____." (Tell children that they can make up words that rhyme.) Then have the other partner do the same with the first child's name. Continue switching partners until everyone has had a chance to learn each student's name. You may wish to take part in the game, also, to make it extra fun for the class and as an aid in learning the names of your students. (This play is also a great activity to perform on Visitors' Day—invite parents, guardians, and other visitors to participate with children.)

We Go to School

WALK OR RIDE?

Before reading this play, take a survey to find out how children in your class get to school. If there are students in each group depicted in the play, have them read that part. If not, let students choose whichever part they like. Later, create a human graph that shows the way students get to school. Have students stand or sit behind one another in rows. (One row consists of walkers, another bus riders, etc.) Ask volunteers to draw a picture to represent each group. Then invite students to step out of their row, one by one, and observe the graph (while you take that student's place in the row). Ask questions, such as, "How do most of the children in our class get to school?" "How do the fewest children get to school?" "How many children take the bus?" and so on.

We Are Your Community

WHO AM I?

Let students brush up their acting skills with this entertaining pantomime activity. First ask them to name the community helpers mentioned in the play. List these on the board. Then ask them to come up with others to add to the list. (store clerk, dentist, newspaper carrier, sanitation worker, druggist, nurse, pizza maker, etc.) Have students then take turns acting out one of these roles while classmates try to guess their identities.

The Magic Place

LOOK FOR A BOOK

Plan a field trip to your local library. Ask a librarian to give your class a tour, so that children learn where to look for favorite books when they visit. If some of your students don't have library cards, take this opportunity to get cards for them. Tell them that their library card is their ticket to the magic place they read about in the play.

Time for Fall

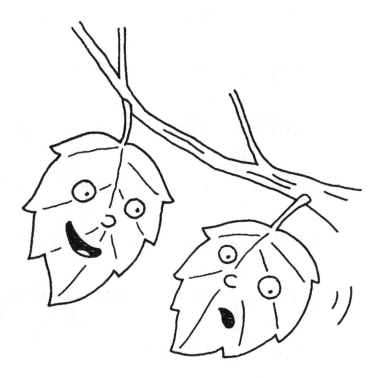

Characters

Leaf 1   Leaf 2

Leaf 1:   Are you ready?

Leaf 2:   I don't think so.

Leaf 1:   Why not?

Leaf 2:   I'm scared.

Leaf 1:   You don't have to be scared.
It will be fun!

Leaf 2:   How do you know?

Leaf 1:   I just do.

Leaf 2:   I still don't know.

Leaf 1:   Just try it.

Leaf 2:   Well, all right.

Leaf 1:   Ready!

Leaf 2:   Set!

Both: Go!

Leaf 1:   Wheeeee! This is fun!

Leaf 2:   Wheeeee! You're right!

Leaf 1:   I am falling nice and slowly.

Leaf 2:   I am blowing in the wind.

Leaf 1:   Are you ready to land?

Leaf 2:   I'm ready.

Leaf 1:   Here we go.

Leaf 2:   What a nice landing!

Leaf 1:   Now I'm tired.

Leaf 2:   So am I.

Leaf 1:   It's time to rest.

Leaf 2:   Sleep well.

The End

Autumn Sounds

Characters

Leaf Cruncher 1	Leaf Cruncher 3	Leaf Cruncher 5
Leaf Cruncher 2	Leaf Cruncher 4	Leaf Cruncher 6

Leaf Cruncher 1:   Crunch! Crunch!
What's that sound?

Leaf Cruncher 2:   Crunch! Crunch!
Look around.

Leaf Cruncher 3:   Crunch! Crunch!
Hear that noise?

Leaf Cruncher 4:   Crunch! Crunch!
Girls and boys?

Leaf Cruncher 5:   Crunch! Crunch!
A mouse with cheese?

Leaf Cruncher 6:   Crunch! Crunch!
It's autumn leaves!

The End

Snowflakes

Characters

Snowflake 1	Snowflake 3	Snowflake 5
Snowflake 2	Snowflake 4	Snowflake 6

Snowflake 1: I am a snowflake.
I look like a flower.

Snowflake 2: I am a snowflake.
I look like a star.

Snowflake 3: I am a snowflake.
I look like a diamond.

25 Just-Right Plays for Emergent Readers Scholastic Professional Books

Snowflake 4:   I am a snowflake.
I look like a cloud.

Snowflake 5:   I am a snowflake.
I look like candy.

Snowflake 6:   I am a snowflake.
I look like a wheel.

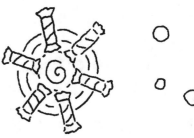

All: We all look different,
But we are all snowflakes.
When we get together.
We make a great snowman!

The End

Groundhog Day

Characters

Groundhog 1   Groundhog 2

Groundhog 1:   Yawn! What a nice long nap!

Groundhog 2:   You are right. I feel great!

Groundhog 1:   I guess we should get up.

Groundhog 2:   Yes. It is time.

Groundhog 1:   I must stretccchhh!

Groundhog 2:   Me, too. stretccchhh! That feels good!

Groundhog 1:   Okay. I'm ready. I'm going out. ················>

    25 Just-Right Plays for Emergent Readers   Scholastic Professional Books

Groundhog 2:   I will wait here.

Groundhog 1:   Remember, if I see my shadow,
                     we will have six more weeks of winter.

Groundhog 2:   And if you don't see it . . .

Both: Time for spring!

Groundhog 1:   See you later.

Groundhog 2:   Good luck!

Groundhog 1:   Up the hole I go. I can see light.
                     I'm almost there. Pop! I am out.*

* To finish the play, read either Ending 1 or Ending 2 ················➤

Ending 1

Groundhog 1: There it is! My shadow!
I must tell my friend.
Down the hole I go.
Hey, friend! Get back in bed.

Groundhog 2: Okay. See you in six weeks.
Good night!

The End

Ending 2

Groundhog 1: Where is my shadow?
I don't see it! I must tell my friend.
Down the hole I go.
Hey, friend! Time to get up!

Groundhog 2: Early spring! Let's go!

The End

Hooray for Spring!

Characters

Spring Lovers 1, 2, 3, 4, 5, 6, 7, 8, 9, 10, 11, and 12

Spring Lover 1:   The winter was icy and snowy.

Spring Lover 2:   The chilly wind made my eyes tear.

Spring Lover 3:   But now we are dancing and singing.

Spring Lovers 1, 2, and 3:   It's spring and we're happy it's here!

Spring Lover 4:   A butterfly sat on my shoulder,

Spring Lover 5:   And told me that summer is near.

Spring Lover 6:   Well, summer is great, but I can wait.

Spring Lovers 4, 5, and 6:   It's spring and we're happy it's here!

................➤

Spring Lover 7:   I love all the beautiful flowers.

Spring Lover 8:   The sky is so sunny and clear.

Spring Lover 9:   The air smells much fresher.
The grass is bright green.

**Spring Lovers
7, 8, and 9:**   It's spring and we're happy it's here!

Spring Lover 10:   While each of the seasons is special,

Spring Lover 11:   There's one that I've wished for
all year.

Spring Lover 12:   Baby birds tweet and
rain makes things grow.

All: It's spring and we're happy it's here!

The End

From Seed to Plant

Characters

Seed / Plant	Water
Soil	Sun

Seed: I am just a little seed.

Someday I hope to be

A healthy, big, and bright green plant

For all the world to see!

Soil: I am the soil. I give the seed

A cozy home to grow in.

I'll keep it warm and snug in March

When the cold wind starts blowin'.

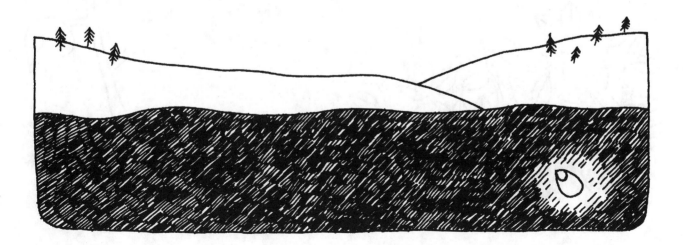

Water: I am water. I will give
The tiny seed a drink.
And then the seed will start to grow
Much sooner than you think!

Sun: I am the sun and my strong rays
Will shine upon the seed.
I'll give it warmth and my bright light,
Both things a plant will need.

Plant: Wow! Look now! I am a plant.
All of you are great at what you do!
Each one of you is special and
I needed every one of you!

The End

Sunflowers

Characters

Sunflower Group 1   Sunflower Group 2

Sunflower Group 1:   We are sunflowers.

Sunflower Group 2:   We look like the sun.

Sunflower Group 1:   We grow in a field.

Sunflower Group 2:   We have lots of fun.

Sunflower Group 1:   We are taller than grass.

Sunflower Group 2:   We are shorter than trees.

Sunflower Group 1:   We have many friends.

Sunflower Group 2:   Our best friends are bees.

Sunflower Group 1:   They visit a lot.

Sunflower Group 2:   And then they go home.

Sunflower Group 1:   Even though they leave,

Sunflower Group 2:   We are not alone.

Sunflower Group 1:   We have each other
as you can see.

Sunflower Group 2:   We are a happy flower family!

The End

Me and My Shadow

Characters

Child	Shadow

Child: Who are you?

Shadow: I am you.

Child: What do you do?

Shadow: I do what you do.

Child: If I move forward,

Shadow: I do, too. ⋯⋯⋯⋯⋯➤

Child: If I move backward,

Shadow: I do, too.

Child: If I jump, jump, jump,

Shadow: I jump, jump, jump, too.

Child: If I run, run, run,

Shadow: I run, run, run, too.

Child: I guess you are a special friend.

Shadow: We will stick together until the end.

Child: I won't be lonely because I have you.

Shadow: I won't be lonely because I have you, too!

The End

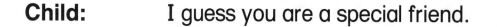

Stormy Weather

Characters

Rain 1	Wind
Rain 2	Lightning
Rain 3	Thunder

Rain 1:   Drip!

Rain 2:   Drop!

Rain 3:   Drip-drop!

Rain 1:   Plink!

Rain 2:   Plonk!

Rain 3:   Plink-plonk!

Wind: Shhhhhhhhh!

Lightning: Crack!   ·····················➤

Thunder: Rumble, rumble.

Wind: Shhhhhhhhh! Whooshhhhhh!

Lightning: Crack!

Thunder: Rumble, rumble.

Rain 1:   Drizzle. Drizzle.

Rain 2:   Drizzle. Drizzle.

Rain 3:   Drizzle. Drizzle.

Wind: Shoosh! Whoosh! Shoosh! Whoosh!

Lightning: Crrr-rack! Crack!

Thunder: Rumble, rumble. Crash! Boom!

Rain 1:   Pitter-patter, pitter-patter.

Rain 2:   Pitter-patter, pitter-patter.

Rain 3:   Pitter-patter, pitter, patter.

Wind: Shhhhh! Whooshhh!

⋯⋯⋯⋯➤

25 Just-Right Plays for Emergent Readers Scholastic Professional Books

Lightning: Crack!

Thunder: Rumble, rumble.

Rain 1:   Drizzle.

Rain 2:   Drizzle.

Rain 3:   Drizzle.

Rain 1:   Plink-plonk!

Rain 2:   Plink!

Rain 3:   Plonk!

Wind: Shhhh!

Rain 1:   Drip-drop.

Rain 2:   Drip.

Rain 3:   Drop.

The End

Neighbors in Space

Characters

The Sun

The Planets: Mercury   Mars   Uranus
              Venus   Jupiter   Neptune
              Earth   Saturn   Pluto

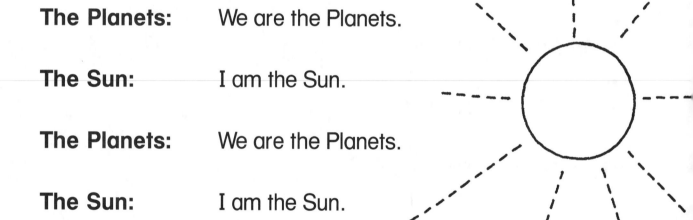

The Planets: We are the Planets.

The Sun: I am the Sun.

The Planets: We are the Planets.

The Sun: I am the Sun.

All: We are neighbors in space!

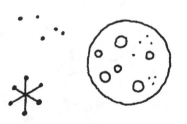

The Sun: I am the Sun.

I am the brightest star in the sky!

All of the planets move around me.

Mercury: I am Mercury.

I live the closest to the sun.

The sun keeps me very warm.

Venus: I am Venus.

People call me the "Evening Star"

because I look so bright!

Earth: Well, you may be bright, but

I am Earth, the only planet full of life!

Mars: Maybe so, but you are not

bright red like me! I am Mars!

Jupiter: Make way for me, mighty Jupiter.

I am the biggest planet of them all!

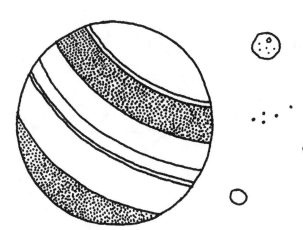

Saturn: I am Saturn, the most beautiful
jewel in the solar system!
Look at all my rings!

Uranus: I am Uranus. I spin sideways.
That makes me different and special.

Neptune: I am Neptune. I am never alone.
I have my little friend Pluto
right beside me all the time!

Pluto: I may be the smallest planet,
but I am also the coldest!
I am Pluto. Brrrrrr!

The Planets: We are the Planets.

The Sun: I am the Sun.

The Planets: We are the Planets.

The Sun: I am the Sun.

All: We are neighbors in space!

The End

Get Set for a Pet

Characters

Fish   Bird   Cat   Dog

All: We are pets
And we're here to say
That we must be cared for
In a special way.

Fish: I am a fish.
I need a clean bowl, fresh water,
fish food, and lots of love.

Bird: I am a bird.
I need a clean cage, fresh water,
bird food, and lots of love.

Cat: I am a cat.
I need a soft bed, fresh water, cat food,
gentle petting, and lots of love.

Dog: I am a dog.
I need a soft bed, fresh water, dog food,
long walks, big hugs, and lots of love.

All: So if you want a pet,
Remember what we say.
We need lots of love
Each and every day!

The End

Guinea Pig Song

Characters

Guinea Pig Friends 1, 2, 3, 4, 5, 6, 7, 8, 9, 10, 11, 12, and 13

Guinea Pig Friend 1:   Guinea pig, guinea pig,
In my lap,

Guinea Pig Friend 2:   Guinea pig, guinea pig,
Take a nap.

Guinea Pig Friend 3:   Guinea pig, guinea pig,
In your cage,

Guinea Pig Friend 4:   Guinea pig, guinea pig,
What's your age?

Guinea Pig Friend 5:   Guinea pig, guinea pig,
On the floor,

Guinea Pig Friend 6:   Guinea pig, guinea pig,
Play some more!

Guinea Pig Friend 7:   Guinea pig, guinea pig,
What's your name?

Guinea Pig Friend 8:   Guinea pig, guinea pig,
Play a game!

Guinea Pig Friend 9:   Guinea pig, guinea pig,
Eat your lunch.

Guinea Pig Friend 10:   Guinea pig, guinea pig,
Munch! Munch! Munch!

Guinea Pig Friend 11:   Guinea pig, guinea pig,
Can you speak?

Guinea Pig Friend 12:   Guinea pig, guinea pig,
Squeak! Squeak! Squeak!

Guinea Pig Friend 13:   Guinea pig, guinea pig,
How do you do?

All: Guinea pig, guinea pig,
We love you!

The End

New Frog in the Pond

Characters

Frog 1   Frog 2

Frog 1:   Who are you?

Frog 2:   I am a frog.

Frog 1:   I am a frog, too.
                Are you new here?

Frog 2:   Yes, I am new.

Frog 1:   Do you like this pond?

Frog 2:   Yes, I like this pond a lot.

Frog 1:   Can you hop?

Frog 2:   Yes, I can hop.

Frog 1:   Show me how you hop.

Frog 2:   Hop! Hop! Hop!

Frog 1:   You are a good hopper!

Frog 2:   Thank you.

Frog 1:   Would you like to be friends?

Frog 2:   Yes, I would like to be friends.

Frog 1:   Let's go hopping.

Both: Hop! Hop! Hop!

The End

A Duckling Tale

Characters

Duckling   Mother Duck

Duckling: Mom, will you please tell me a story?

Mother Duck: Yes, my duckling.
What story do you want to hear?

Duckling: Tell me about when I was born.

Mother Duck: Okay. You were inside
a small, white egg.
I sat on the egg to keep it warm.

Duckling:	How did I get food?
Mother Duck:	All the food you needed was inside the egg.
Duckling:	Then what happened?
Mother Duck:	One day, you cracked the eggshell with your tiny beak.
Duckling:	I was ready to come out!
Mother Duck:	Yes. You pecked and pecked at the shell. That's how you hatched out of the egg!
Duckling:	What happened next?
Mother Duck:	You became my fuzzy little duckling!
Duckling:	Mom?
Mother Duck:	Yes, my duckling.
Duckling:	I'm glad I hatched.
Mother Duck:	So am I, my duckling.

The End

25 Just-Right Plays for Emergent Readers Scholastic Professional Books

Fish School

Characters

Ms. Fish	Student Fish 1	Student Fish 3
	Student Fish 2	Student Fish 4

Ms. Fish: Good morning, class!

All Student Fish: Good morning, Ms. Fish!

Ms. Fish: Today we will go over our fish school rules. What do we do if we have something to say?

Student Fish 1: We raise our fins!

Ms. Fish: Right. How do we sit at our desks?

Student Fish 2: With our tails on the floor.

Ms. Fish: Very good. What if you bring in a snack of worms?

Student Fish 3: Make sure you bring enough worms to share with everyone.

Ms. Fish: Yes. What if someone makes you mad?

Student Fish 4: You should try to talk it out. Don't blow bubbles in someone's face!

Ms. Fish: Excellent work! Now, what would you like to learn about today?

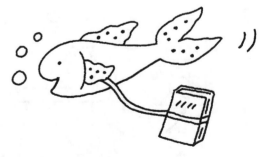

All Student Fish: People!

The End

Ready to Fly

Characters

Bird 1   Bird 2   Bird 3   Bird 4

Bird 1:   Brrrr! It's getting cold here up north!
                I guess it's time to go.

Bird 2:   Time to go where?

Bird 3:   South, silly! That's what we birds do.

Bird 4:   When it starts to get cold up here,
                we fly down south where it's warm.

Bird 2:   What should I bring?

Bird 1: Just yourself.
Get ready to eat a lot of bugs, too!

Bird 2: Bugs! Yummy!
But why do we have to fly south to eat bugs?

Bird 3: Many bugs die when it gets cold.
But there are plenty of bugs down south
where it's warm!

Bird 2: That sounds great! Let's stay there forever.

Bird 4: We can't. In a few months,
it will get cold down south.

Bird 1: And it will get warm up north.

Bird 2: So we'll fly back here?
What about the bugs?

Bird 3: There will be many bugs here again
once the weather gets warm.

Bird 2: I see. Warm weather and bugs.
What are we waiting for? Let's go!

The End

D Is for Dinosaur

Characters

Tanya   Sam   Ruby

Tanya: D is for dinosaur.

Sam: D is for dinosaur.

Ruby: D is for dinosaur.

All: Yes it is!

Tanya: Have you ever seen a dinosaur?

Sam: No. I've never seen a dinosaur.
You can't see a dinosaur.
They are all extinct.

Ruby: I've seen a dinosaur.

Tanya: You have not!

Ruby: Yes, I have.
I saw a dinosaur yesterday. ·············▸

Sam: Where did you see it?

Ruby: I went to a museum.
That's where I saw it.
It's a big and bony dinosaur.
Its name is Tyrannosaurus Rex!

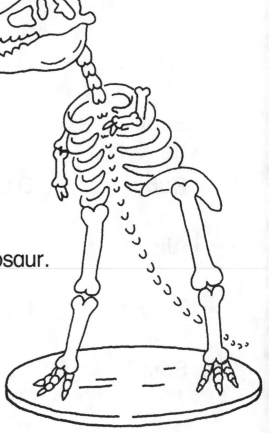

**Tanya
and Sam:** Wow!

Ruby: Do you want to see
the dinosaur?

Tanya: Yes, I want to see it!

Sam: Let's go and see the dinosaur.

All: Let's go now!

Tanya: D is for dinosaur.

Sam: D is for dinosaur.

Ruby: D is for dinosaur.

All: Yes it is!

The End

Pop! Pop! Popcorn!

··

Characters

Popcorn 1, 2, 3, 4, 5, 6, and 7

Popcorn 1: Pop!

Popcorn 2: Pop!

Popcorn 3: Pop! Pop!

Popcorn 4: Pop! Pop!

Popcorn 5: Pop! Pop! Pop!

Popcorn 6: Pop! Pop! Pop!

Popcorn 7: Pip!

**Popcorns
1 to 6:** Pip?

Popcorn 7: Pop!

The End

Big, Bad Cold

Characters

Sniffles	Cough	Fever
Sneeze	Sore Throat	

Sniffles: I am the sniffles.
Sniff! Sniff! Sniff!

Sneeze: I am a sneeze.
Achoo! Achoo! Achoo!

Cough: I am a cough.
Cough! Cough! Cough!

Sore Throat: I am a sore throat.
Ow! Ow! Ow!

Fever: I am a fever.
Hot! Hot! Hot!

All: Put us all together.
What do you have?
A big, bad cold!

The End

Loose Tooth

Characters

Nick	Raj
Mi Won	Ana
Jerome	

Nick: Hey everyone!
Look what I have. My mom gave me
some red, crunchy apples!

Mi Won: Apples! Yum!

Jerome: May I have one, please?

Raj: Me, too?

Nick: Sure. There are enough apples
for everyone.

Ana: I can't have one.

Mi Won: Why not?

Ana: I have a loose tooth.

Nick: A loose tooth! That's great!

Ana: Why is that great?

Jerome: That means you are growing up.

Ana: It does? Wow!

Raj: Just wait a while and that tooth will come out.

Nick: Then, a new and bigger tooth will grow in the same place!

Ana: That's great! Then I can eat all of the apples I want. Look out, apples! Here I come!

The End

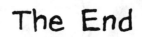

25 Just-Right Plays for Emergent Readers Scholastic Professional Books

Time for the Party!

Characters

Birthday Child	Cake	Ice Cream	Friends
Balloons	Candles	Gifts	

Birthday Child: Today is my birthday.
I have everything I need
for a great birthday party!

Balloons: We are balloons.
We are colorful and fun!

Cake: I am a cake.
I am covered with frosting!

Candles: We are candles.
We will tell how old you are.

Ice Cream: I am ice cream.
I am cold and yummy!

Gifts: We are gifts.
We will give you a nice surprise!

Birthday Child: Well, time for the party.
But, wait. Something is missing.

Balloons: You have balloons.

Cake: You have cake.

Candles: You have candles.

Ice Cream: You have ice cream.

Gifts: You have gifts.

Birthday child: What is missing?

Friends: Friends!

All: Time for the party!

The End

The Name Game

Characters

Name Game Players (as many players as you wish)

All: We all have names.
We all love games.
This is called
The Name Game.

Name Game Player 1: My name is _____.
That rhymes with _____.

Name Game Player 2: My name is _____.
That rhymes with _____.

................→

Name Game Player 3:   My name is _____.
                            That rhymes with _____.

Name Game Player 4:   My name is _____.
                            That rhymes with _____.

Name Game Player 5:   My name is _____.
                            That rhymes with _____.

(Continue the game until all players have had a turn.)

All: These are our names.
                            No two are the same.
                            We hope you liked
                            Our little Name Game!

The End

We Go to School

Bus Group: We go riding on a bus,
On a bus,
On a bus.
We go riding on a bus.
That's how we get to school.

Bicycle Group: We go riding on our bikes,
On our bikes,
On our bikes.
We go riding on our bikes.
That's how we get to school.

Car Group: We go riding in a car,
In a car,
In a car.
We go riding in a car.
That's how we get to school.

Walking Group: We go walking with our feet,
With our feet,
With our feet.
We go walking with our feet.
That's how we get to school.

All: No matter how we get to school,
Get to school,
Get to school,
No matter how we get to school,
We love coming to school!

The End

We Are Your Community

Characters

Child	Firefighter	Librarian	Friends
Police Officer	Teacher	Mail Carrier	

Child: I just moved to this new place.
I wonder who else lives here?

All Others: Community, community.
We are your community.
Community, community.
We will help you like it here. You'll see!

Police Officer: I am a police officer.
I will help keep you safe. ················▶

Firefighter: I am a firefighter.
I will put out fires.

Teacher: I am a teacher.
I will help you learn new things.

Librarian: I am a librarian.
I will help you find good books to read.

Mail Carrier: I am a mail carrier.
I will bring you letters.

Friends: We are friends.
We will help you feel welcome.

Child: Wow! I think I will like it here!
I'm glad to live in this community!

The End

The Magic Place

Characters

Luke   Maria   Tamika   Seth

Luke: Hey! Where are you going?

Maria: We are going to a magic place.

Luke: What kind of magic place?

Tamika: A place that can take us anywhere and show us anything!

Luke: What do you mean?

Seth: We can visit China or Africa.

Maria: We can meet George Washington
               or Mother Goose!

Tamika: Want to come with us?

Luke: I don't know. It sounds kind of scary.

Seth: Don't be scared.
               This magic place is wonderful!

Luke: Well, okay. Let's go.

Maria: Here we are!

Luke: Hey, this is the library.

Tamika: Yes. It is our magic place.

Seth: With all the books here, we can go
               anywhere and meet anyone.

Luke: Well, what are we waiting for?
               Let's go inside!

The End